The LoveSpell Secret

A 30-Day Heaven-Sent Program to
Create More Love in Your Life

I. J. Weinstock

© 2013 by DreaMasters, Inc.

All Rights Reserved

For information write:

DreaMaster Books
17130 Burbank Blvd.
Suite 302
Encino, CA 91316

Online at:

www.DreaMasterBooks.com

Book design services provided by
EditWriteDesign.com

No part of this book may be reproduced or transmitted in any form or by any means, graphic, electronic, or mechanical, including photocopying, recording, taping, or by any information storage retrieval system, without the written permission of the publisher.

Praise for the
The LoveSpell Secret

"What do you love?" What a profound and necessary question. Thanks for reminding us to ask the question on a regular basis. To paraphrase the wisdom in this handbook, I think we'd all do well to acknowledge, appreciate and pay attention to this guide!

— Dr. Seth Kadish
"Pop Your Patterns: *The No-Nonsense Way to Change Your Life*"

I am blown away about how beautiful this concept is and how ingenious because I know that it works!

— Carol A

*What you have created is just amazing!!!
Thank you for this wonderful gift that
will certainly make a difference in my life!!!*

— Marie De Keersmaeker

What the world needs is more love. "The LoveSpell Secret" shows you step-by-step how to have more love in all areas of your life. You will have your eyes and hearts open to a new level of understanding of how deep (and easy) love can be. This is a great opportunity to shift your perception from one of fear to one of love in all you do.

— Kathleen Gage

Awesome! Much truth and revelation!!

— Sylvene B.

This little handbook is short and sweet. And so good for you:-) It's like a teaspoon of sugar that helps with the difficult task of re-calibrating one's perspective. Though it's a small book, the message is an important one. Reading a portion of it everyday will give one an opportunity to gently, slowly, refocus one's vision...opening a portal to their own beauty and love and the love that surrounds them.

— Angel

Doing the simple daily exercise in your book trains our chatty and unruly minds to focus—focus away from the daily grind and unproductive thoughts that have a stranglehold on our minds— onto feelings and ideas that will reduce stress and ultimately enrich our lives. Even just a handful of minutes a day will, I'm sure, begin to slowly improve one's life. Thank you!

— Tatiana P.

What an amazing little gem of a book...thank you! I thought I'd write just a few of them to get me started...but here I am up to 90 in one sitting and still going strong! So I thought I'd take a moment just to let you know how much I appreciate this little gift at this time. It's a simple plan and that's the best kind since it addresses the most profound areas of the soul. I think I love it! Thank you again!

— Diane

Sweet & easy read to get you to think playfully about what you love. It leaps joyfully from silliness like loving wearing a red clown nose to make children laugh, to the depth of loving the interconnectedness of all humans breathing the same air. And it's a great little happiness fitness program to increase what we love through daily appreciation.

— Suzanne S.

For Joy, Lilly & My Mother—
Three wonderful women who've taught me
most of what I know about Love.

*May your life be filled with love &
may you fill the world with your love!*

— I. J. Weinstock

*And in the end the love you take
is equal to the love you make*

— **the Beatles**

Love is the Answer

Poets and philosophers sing the praises of love. Even the Bible proclaims *Love is the answer*. I discovered the profound truth, of what for many is a cliché, in the most unlikely way.

On New Year's Eve I attended a drum circle to ring in 2012. I sat in a Long Island living room with a dozen other people, beating a hand-held Native American drum in the traditional heartbeat rhythm. Ba*bam*...ba*bam*. The room vibrated with the booming beat of the 12 drums which mimicked our hearts and soon became hypnotic. That's when it happened—I heard my late wife, Joy, ask me a question which changed my life.

This wasn't the first time I'd received supernatural communications from the Afterlife. In fact, I wrote an award-winning memoir about how Joy helped heal my grief entitled, *JOYride: How My Late Wife Loved Me Back To Life.*

The question Joy asked me on that fateful New Year's Eve was simple yet profound: *What do you love?* As if in answer, I began beating the drum for all the things that I loved. With each drumbeat I silently declared:

- I love ceremony and celebration.
- I love being among kindred spirits.
- I love banging a drum!

By the end of the drum circle, I'd made a new year's resolution to *beat the drum for love* all year. For me, 2012 would be *The Year of Love*. On January 1st, via my Twitter account @SoulmateGuider, I began *beating the drum for love:*

- **I love candlelight, moonlight, the spotlight.**
- **I love walking, stretching, dancing.**
- **I love a good yawn, a loud sigh & a deep breath.**

Every day I declared something else I loved, and began to notice a subtle shift taking place within me. I became more aware of just how many things I loved.

I began collecting loves like beautiful seashells on a beach. And the more loves I found, the more I began to see. The more I saw, the better I felt.

- **I love wearing a red clown nose to make children happy.**
- **I love the word "and" because it's the most hopeful word in the English language.**
- **I love LOSING myself in the dance & FINDING myself in the stillness of meditation**

I calculated that by the end of 2012, I'll collect, inventory and catalog at least 1001 loves.

- **I love watching the ducks, geese & egrets at the lake.**
- **I love squeezing the last bit of toothpaste out of the tube for days and even weeks.**
- **I love remembering great memories from my past, my passions and even my passwords**

With each love declaration, I felt enriched, as if I was putting money in the bank. A *LoveBank*! What if I deposit ten thousand loves? A hundred thousand? What would it feel like to be a *Love-illionaire?*

- **I love standing up for myself, for another, for what's right.**
- **I love playing with children & being child-like with adults.**
- **I love seeing old friends and getting caught up on their new adventures.**

To inspire others the way Joy had inspired me, my 140-character tweets also contained her question: ***WhatDoULove?***

- **I love hearing bird song, cricket choirs & whale symphonies.** *WhatDoULove?*
- **I love getting so quiet that I can feel the blood rushing through my veins.** *WhatDoULove?*
- **I love arriving home after a long trip and falling into bed.** *WhatDoULove?*

Something powerful was happening. *Beating the drum for love* felt like a chant, a prayer, an incantation. So I began doing some research hoping to understand what I was experiencing.

*Because what you focus on expands,
when you focus on the goodness in your life,
you create more of it.*

— **Oprah Winfrey**

The Quantum Effect

Metaphysics and quantum physics both maintain that whatever you put your attention on expands. In the same way that a magnifying glass makes everything appear bigger or can focus the rays of the sun to ignite a fire, whatever you focus your awareness on grows.

Neuroscience has confirmed that when you become consciously aware of any enjoyment, you amplify and magnify the experience. Think of it as scientific validation for the prescription to *count your blessings.*

Other studies have demonstrated that important life skills such as love and happiness can be learned in the same way one learns to play a musical instrument, a sport or a game like chess. With practice, the mental and physical moves become automatic. The brain can be trained. Certain states of mind and positive emotions, like love and happiness, can be cultivated. But like any skill, it requires practice until it's mastered.

From my research, I realized that Joy's question—*What do you love?*—had given me a magical key to open the treasure chest of life. But it's my daily declarations of love which create a magical spell—a *LoveSpell*—that expands the love in my life. With Joy's help I'd stumbled upon one of the secrets to life. And now I'm excited to share the magic and power of *The LoveSpell Secret* with you.

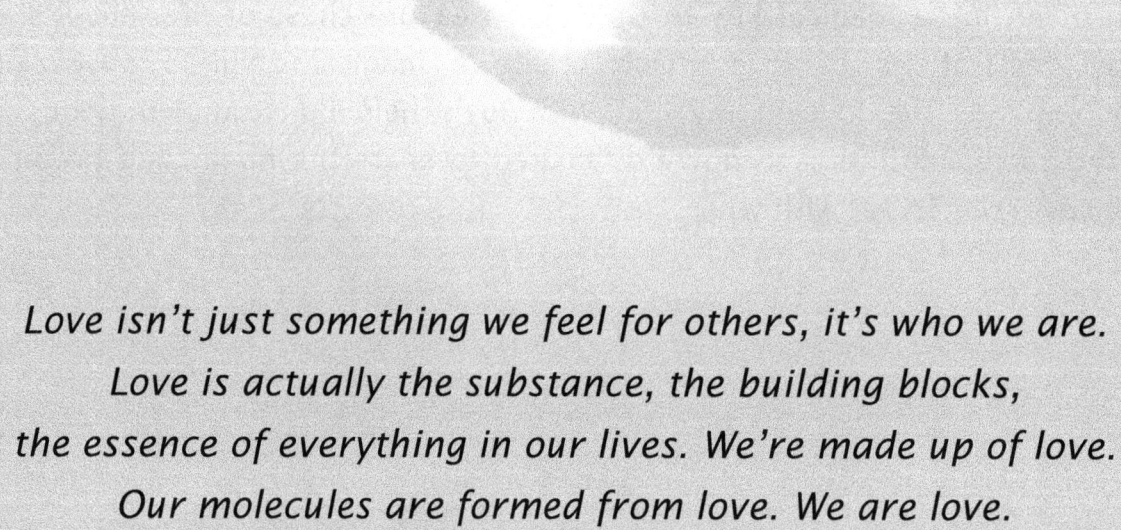

*Love isn't just something we feel for others, it's who we are.
Love is actually the substance, the building blocks,
the essence of everything in our lives. We're made up of love.
Our molecules are formed from love. We are love.*

— **Marci Shimoff**

The LoveSpell Secret

The message of religion, philosophy and countless pop songs boils down to one simple truth—*Love is the Answer*. For many people that simplistic idea is nothing more than a sentimental cliché. But like some fairy tale, the real secret is hidden within an Alice-in-Wonderland-like paradox. For if you take the cliché, *"Love is the Answer"* and turn it around so that *"Love is the Question,"* you'll have discovered the hidden secret and will possess a magical key to transform your life.

By answering the question—*What do you love?*—you activate the magic of *The LoveSpell Secret* and benefit from the quantum effect.

When you *Cast a Quantum LoveSpell*, you're "mining" your life for the "gold" of the things you love and become enriched.

By *Acknowledging*, *Appreciating* and paying *Attention* to what you love—in other words, triple *AAA-ing* your loves—you cultivate and actually *grow* the love in your life.

Whoever discovers *The LoveSpell Secret* holds the magic key to unlock the treasure chest of their life.

We are all born for love.
It is the principle of existence, and its only end.

— **Benjamin Disraeli**

I Love, Therefore I Am!

It's been said that when we face death, our wealth, our success, even the knowledge we've gained over a lifetime matters little. What remains in those last precious moments of life is the singular realization of the importance of love. Ultimately, it is love that defines us—*I love, therefore I am!*

A friend, after being pronounced dead for nearly a half-hour, returned from her near-death experience proclaiming, *Love is all there is!*

The ancient Egyptians believed that after we die, our souls undergo a life-review in which we're asked two questions: *Did you love? Were you loved?*

Questions are the key. Whether we realize it or not, our lives are a result of asking questions that propel us on quests to answer them. The questions we ask determine the quest we take.

What do you love? is one of the most important questions you can ask yourself. The more you answer that question, the more love you will discover on your life's quest.

Love is indeed the Answer. But that's only partly true. *The LoveSpell Secret* provides the missing part—Love is also the Question.

The hunger for love is much more difficult to remove than the hunger for bread.

— **Mother Teresa**

Vitamin L Deficiency

Most people suffer from a Vitamin Love deficiency. This is partly due to an innate survival instinct in humans that programs us to focus on and pay attention to what's *wrong* with a situation. This programming has an evolutionary advantage—it guarantees survival.

If you need any proof, just look at the news. Though there's lots of good news, we're bombarded with bad news by a media whose mission statement is: "If it bleeds, it leads!" Why? Because bad news gets ratings. The media manipulates our survival programming to focus on "what's wrong" in order to attract viewers and ultimately profits.

Since we all suffer, to one degree or another, from a Vitamin L deficiency that has profound consequences on our health and happiness, the single greatest gift you can give yourself is a daily dose of Vitamin Love.

Love sets off a set of physiological events in the body: peptides and hormones are released, including endorphins, oxytocin, dopamine, vasopressin, and nitric oxide. These help turn off the fear response, evoke the relaxation response and create a positive physiology.

— Dr. Eva Selhub, Harvard Medical School
(in *Love For No Reason* by Marci Shimoff)

The Amazing Benefits of Vitamin L

Research has demonstrated that Vitamin L has amazing health and wellness benefits. Studies have shown that love, in many cases, can heal as powerfully as medicine.

Vitamin L can make you smarter, help fight cancer, as well as strengthen your immune, endocrine and cardiovascular systems. Vitamin L can lower your cholesterol as well as your blood pressure, reduce pain, and speed the healing of an injury. Sounds like a wonder drug? It just might be!

And here's one of the reasons why. In his groundbreaking book, "Messages from Water," Dr Masaru Emoto used powerful electron microscopes to capture newly formed crystals in frozen water samples and discovered that *water reacts to our thoughts, words and emotions.*

According to Dr. Emoto, thoughts, prayers, music and meditation, transmit vibrations to water that affects the way it crystallizes. Water exposed to loving words showed brilliant, complex, and beautiful crystals. In contrast, water influenced by negative thoughts or words formed incomplete, asymmetrical, ugly crystals. The most beautiful water crystals, Dr. Emoto said, were formed when they were exposed to the words or emotion of *Love*.

The human body is more than 60% water. Our blood is 92% water, our brain and muscles are 75%, and even our bones are about 22% water. Whenever you think about what you love, the water in you experiences this magical purifying and beautifying effect. Call it *LoveRx*.

*Trust in what you love, continue to do it,
and it will take you where you need to go.*

— Natalie Goldberg

Casting a Quantum Love Spell

Casting a Quantum LoveSpell is a simple yet powerful practice that will grow the love in your life. If you "mine" your life for the "gold" of all the things you love, you'll discover how rich you truly are.

Remember, whatever you focus on grows. So why not focus on what you love! When you *Cast a Quantum LoveSpell*, you sow the seeds of love and reap the benefits of a happier and healthier life that Vitamin L provides.

If you're in a relationship, *Casting a Quantum LoveSpell* will upgrade the *in-to-me-see*, better known as intimacy.

If you're single and looking for that special someone, one of the secrets to finding a soulmate is to grow the love in your life and become more love-*able*—in other words, *able to love. Casting a Quantum LoveSpell* is a daily workout that will build your Love Muscle.

Even mothers-to-be will benefit. And so will their children. Wouldn't it be wonderful if expectant mothers grew the love in their life while growing the baby in their womb.

The LoveSpell Secret is so simple even a child can do it. In fact, children *should* do it. It's as important for them as learning to brush their teeth. Parents who teach their children the habit of focusing on what they love, give them an invaluable life skill whose benefits are incalculable. Our happiness, to a large measure, is a result of the way we view the world. If we've learned to see *the glass as half-empty*, we feel different than if we see *the glass as half-full*. Parents who teach their children to focus on what they love, help them see their glass as half-full no matter the circumstances.

Playing the *LoveSpell Game* with your child—at the kitchen table, while putting them to bed, or in the car—will not only make them happier, it's a fun way to train them to look at life through "love-colored glasses." If they master the *LoveSpell Game* as children, they'll reap the amazing benefits that a daily dose of Vitamin L provides for the rest of their lives.

*Love doesn't just sit there, like a stone.
It has to be made, like bread;
re-made all the time, made new.*

— Ursula LeGuin

The 30-Day LoveSpell Program

To *Cast a Quantum LoveSpell* just answer the question *What do you love?* Like brushing your teeth, do it every day. If you do it for a month, you'll have developed a habit—*a Love habit*. When you've developed the habit of looking at your life through *love-colored glasses*, you'll find that the view is amazing!

The LoveSpell Secret's 30-day program will help you Acknowledge, Appreciate and pay Attention to the love that's already in your life. By *triple-AAAing* what you love, you'll be making deposits in your *LoveBank* that make you feel richer every day.

But to actually grow the love in your life, you can't just read about it, you have to actually do it. If for the next 30 days you *Cast a Quantum LoveSpell* by declaring what you love, you will receive the amazing benefits of your increased dose of Vitamin L. And you will have learned that the power to grow the love in your life is in your hands. And in your heart. So let's begin….

To the Too-Busy, Already-Loves-Themselves Reader in All of Us:

You don't learn to dance, play the piano or hit a golf ball by watching a video. Understanding principles and gaining knowledge isn't enough. Knowing is not doing. Would you expect to get into physical shape by reading a book?

If you've ever mastered anything, you did so by practice, by repetition, by exercising certain actions until they became effortless and automatic. *Casting a Quantum LoveSpell* re-programs your innate survival instinct that pays attention to what's *wrong* to instead focus on what's *right*. But until you actually do the exercise, you'll never see any results.

Also, doing ninety "I love's…" in one sitting (as one enthusiastic *LoveSpeller* did) is great, but doesn't take the place of doing one or two a day. Habits are created by repetition. What we do a-lot-of *sometimes* is not nearly as powerful as what we do a-little-of *all the time*. It's not what you do sometimes, but what you do every day that makes a difference in your life. It's the habit that casts the spell! So let's begin….

Happiness is anyone and anything that's loved by you.

— **Charles M. Schulz**

I love swinging a tennis racket, a baseball bat & my dance partner.

WhatDoULove? I ♥ _____

_____

_____

_____

I love the people in my life
who scratch an itch I can't reach.

WhatDoULove? I ♥ _____

_____

_____

_____

*Love is everywhere but most of us are blind to it.
Romance is just one aspect of love.
Our primary relationship is with ourselves.*

— Marianne Williamson

I love finding money—pennies in the street or checks in the mail.

WhatDoULove? I ♥ _____

_____

_____

_____

I love feeding the ducks & geese & seagulls at the Lake, even though you're not supposed to.

WhatDoULove? I ♥ _____

_____

_____

_____

*Love the animals, love the plants, love everything.
If you love everything,
you will perceive the divine mystery.*

— Dostoyevsky

I love seeing lightning bugs flash on
& off in the dusk.

WhatDoULove? I ♥ _____

_____

_____

_____

I love starting up conversations with strangers
and discovering what we have in common.

WhatDoULove? I ♥ _____

_____

_____

_____

Love life and life will love you back.

— Arthur Rubinstein

Day 4

I love swinging on my hammock,
feeling soothed as if rocked in a cradle.

WhatDoULove? I ♥ _____

_____

_____

_____

I love exercising my body and my imagination,
but not at the same time.

WhatDoULove? I ♥ _____

_____

_____

_____

Love your neighbor as yourself — *Leviticus 19:18*
Even the Bible proclaims this the supreme commandment.
But the Golden Rule begins with us...and what we love.

— I. J Weinstock

I love blowing bubbles for the children in my life & the child in me.

WhatDoULove? I ♥ _____

_____

_____

_____

I love eggs: scrambled, omelet, over-easy, even huevos rancheros.

WhatDoULove? I ♥ _____

_____

_____

_____

Love is the master key which opens the gates of happiness.

— Oliver Wendell Holmes

I love the silence of early morning's birdsong before the noise of my To Do's.

WhatDoULove? I ♥ _____

_____

_____

_____

I love listening to music with my hips, leaving big tips, and watching a beautiful woman apply color to her lips.

WhatDoULove? I ♥ _____

_____

_____

_____

Every single one of us can do things that no one else can do, can love things that on one else can love.

— **Barbara Sher**

I love yawning, howling, Wow-ing.
I love breathtaking moments.

WhatDoULove? I ♥ _____

_____

_____

_____

I love seeing old friends, hearing their good news
& celebrating someone's dream-come-true.

WhatDoULove? I ♥ _____

_____

_____

_____

Reflections & Aha's

Week 1

*Only one thing has to change
for us to know happiness in our lives:
where we focus our attention.*

— **Greg Anderson**

Day 8

I love seeing the first buds of the cherry blossoms.

WhatDoULove? I ♥ _____

_____

_____

_____

I love being wise about some things and silly about others.

WhatDoULove? I ♥ _____

_____

_____

_____

The LoveSpell Secret 35

Love absolutely everything that ever happens in your life.

— **Paul Cantalupo**

I love movies that surprise me,
yet I love seeing some movies again & again.

WhatDoULove? I ♥ _____

_____

_____

_____

I love birds in flight, Lady Justice doing right,
and the pen making might.

WhatDoULove? I ♥ _____

_____

_____

_____

If only you could love enough, you would be the happiest and most powerful being in the universe.

— **Emmet Fox**

I love the way a sunny day feels after a rainy one.

WhatDoULove? I ♥ _____

_____

_____

_____

I love "synchronicities" or as some people call them "coincidences."

WhatDoULove? I ♥ _____

_____

_____

_____

Whenever we love, we are creating Heaven on Earth.

— **I. J. Weinstock**

I love full moons, especially at moonrise
when it looks so incredibly big!

WhatDoULove? I ♥ _____

_____

_____

_____

I love stretching in the shower
while the hot water massages my muscles.

WhatDoULove? I ♥ _____

_____

_____

_____

Life is a conspiracy to shower you with a nonstop feast of interesting experiences, all of which are designed to help you grow your intelligence, shed your pretensions, and master the art of ingenious love.

— Rob Brezsny

Day 12

I love every time I can see the half-empty glass as half-full, better yet full, and even overflowing.

WhatDoULove? I ♥ _____

_____

_____

_____

I love having friends over for dinner and getting drunk on our laughter.

WhatDoULove? I ♥ _____

_____

_____

_____

*The heart is like a garden.
It can grow compassion or fear, resentment or love.
What seeds will you plant there?*

— Jack Kornfield

I love the strength I get from being loved and the courage I get from loving someone.

WhatDoULove? I ♥ _____

_____

_____

_____

I love when my eyes water with emotion because it feels like my tears are watering the garden of my soul.

WhatDoULove? I ♥ _____

_____

_____

_____

*There is no such thing as an idle thought.
All thought creates form on some level.
Every thought leads to either love or fear.*

— **A Course in Miracles**

I love sharing the good times
because it multiplies it.

WhatDoULove? I ♥ _____

_____

_____

_____

I love being so full of my own life
that I don't have time
to watch my favorite TV programs.

WhatDoULove? I ♥ _____

_____

_____

_____

Reflections & Aha's

Week 2

*We are all born for love.
It is the principle of existence, and its only end.*

— **Benjamin Disraeli**

I love buying EXPERIENCES rather than THINGS—
that's how I grow my soul.

WhatDoULove? I ♥ _____

_____

_____

_____

I love hearing from old friends
and "reeling in the years."

WhatDoULove? I ♥ _____

_____

_____

_____

Happiness is love, nothing else.

— Herman Hesse

I love jumping on my trampoline in the morning 108 times.

WhatDoULove? I ♥ _____

_____

_____

_____

I love taking a nap on a rainy day.

WhatDoULove? I ♥ _____

_____

_____

_____

Let yourself be silently drawn by the stronger pull of what you really love.

— **Rumi**

I love watching my team win especially when they come from behind.

WhatDoULove? I ♥ _____

_____

_____

_____

I love rolling on the floor with children & laughing til it hurts.

WhatDoULove? I ♥ _____

_____

_____

_____

Eventually you will come to understand that love heals everything, and love is all there is.

— **Gary Zukav**

I love eating popcorn in the movies and getting the salt just right.

WhatDoULove? I ♥ _____

_____

_____

_____

I love the sound of the ocean as the waves crash upon the shore.

WhatDoULove? I ♥ _____

_____

_____

_____

We are shaped and fashioned by what we love.

— **Goethe**

I love stroking my beard, rubbing my palms together, and scratching my head.

WhatDoULove? I ♥ _____

_____

_____

_____

I love looking through old photos and remembering where and who I've been... and with whom.

WhatDoULove? I ♥ _____

_____

_____

_____

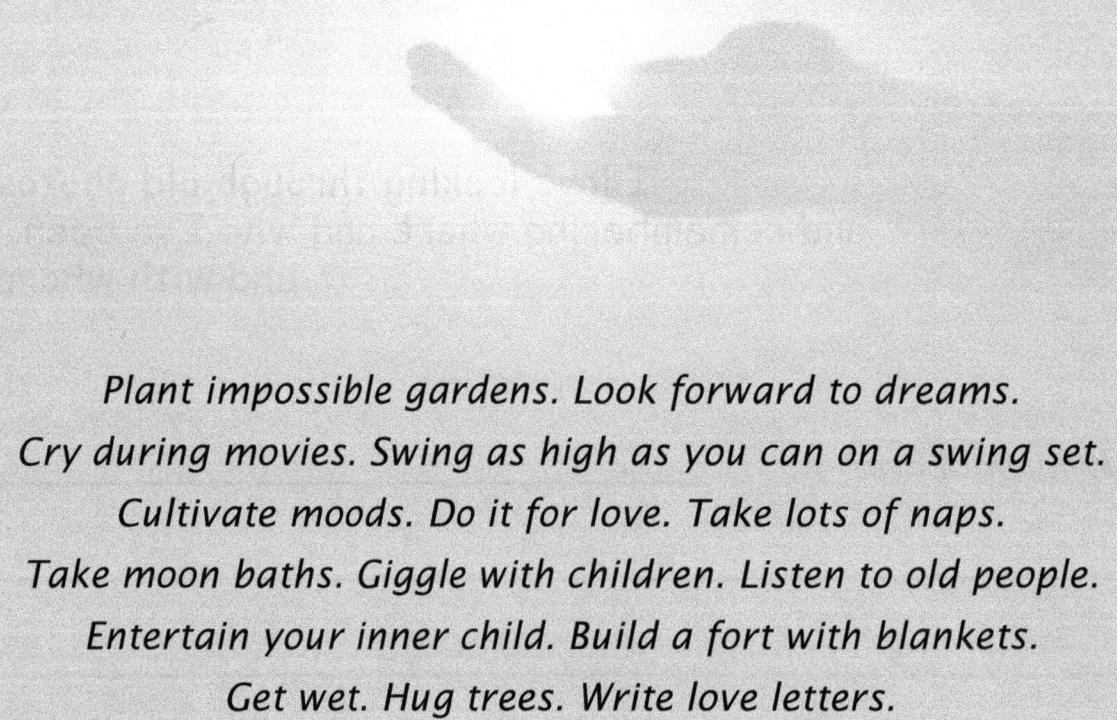

*Plant impossible gardens. Look forward to dreams.
Cry during movies. Swing as high as you can on a swing set.
Cultivate moods. Do it for love. Take lots of naps.
Take moon baths. Giggle with children. Listen to old people.
Entertain your inner child. Build a fort with blankets.
Get wet. Hug trees. Write love letters.*

— Sark

I love finding a parking space,
and fitting even more dishes into the dishwasher
after someone else thinks it's full.

WhatDoULove? I ♥ _____

_____

_____

_____

_____

I love flipping through books I've read and reading the
highlighted passages that remind me
what I thought important then.

WhatDoULove? I ♥ _____

_____

_____

_____

_____

*We are made by love, we are made of love,
and we are made for love! Everything is love anyway.
Our hate is love turned sour, jealousy is love turned bitter,
our fears are love standing upside down,
greed is love gone overboard, attachment is love gone sticky.*

— Khurshed Batliwala

Day 21

I love a good yawn, a loud sigh
& a deep breath.

WhatDoULove? I ♥ _____

_____

_____

_____

I love having my feet on the ground,
my head in the clouds & the sun on my face.

WhatDoULove? I ♥ _____

_____

_____

_____

Reflections & Aha's

Week 3

*Love is the joy of the good,
the wonder of the wise,
the amazement of the Gods.*

— Plato

Day 22

I love my capacity to feel profoundly,
both love AND loss.

WhatDoULove? I ♥ _____

_____

_____

_____

I love finding feathers on the ground and
walking the beach for hours collecting seashells.

WhatDoULove? I ♥ _____

_____

_____

_____

*As I grow to understand life less and less,
I learn to love it more and more.*

— Jules Renard

I love licking ice cream from a cone, especially jamoca almond fudge

WhatDoULove? I ♥ _____

_____

_____

_____

I love hearing good news
and how truly remarkable people are.

WhatDoULove? I ♥ _____

_____

_____

_____

*The happy man is he who lives the life of love,
not for the honors it may bring, but for the life itself.*

— R.J. Baughan

I love the sound of chimes,
the smell of thyme
& the satisfaction of rhymes.

WhatDoULove? I ♥ _____

_____

_____

_____

I love 4-letter words like Hope, True, Care,
Kind, Give and, of course, Love.

WhatDoULove? I ♥ _____

_____

_____

_____

*Love is the great miracle cure.
Loving ourselves works miracles in our lives.*

— Louise Hay

Day 26

I love being intoxicated by the fragrance of night-blooming jasmine.

WhatDoULove? I ♥ _____

_____

_____

_____

I love Reese's peanut butter cups and Mounds more than Almond Joy.

WhatDoULove? I ♥ _____

_____

_____

_____

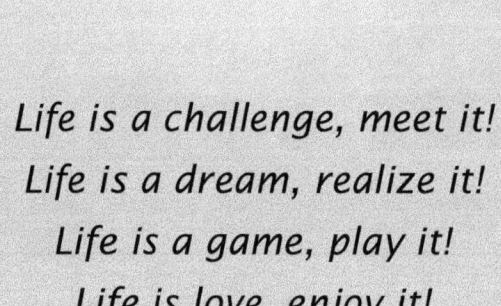

Life is a challenge, meet it!
Life is a dream, realize it!
Life is a game, play it!
Life is love, enjoy it!

— Sai Baba

I love my car—the reliability, convenience & freedom it gives me.

WhatDoULove? I ♥ _____

_____

_____

_____

I love Fridays—TGIF—
a feeling of completion & anticipation.

WhatDoULove? I ♥ _____

_____

_____

_____

*We are like violins.
We can be used for doorstops, or we can make music.
The first step is to find out what you love.*

— Barbara Sher

I love eating comfort foods like garlic mashed potatoes and meatloaf.

WhatDoULove? I ♥ _____

_____

_____

_____

I love listening to music with my butt instead of my ears & moving to the rhythm.

WhatDoULove? I ♥ _____

_____

_____

_____

I ♥

I ♥

I ♥

I ♥

I ♥

I ♥

I ♥

Reflections & Aha's

Week 4

The moment you have in your heart this extraordinary thing called love and feel the depth, the delight, the ecstasy of it, you will discover that for you the world is transformed.

— **Krishnamurti**

Day 29

I love getting good news,
especially when it's unexpected.

WhatDoULove? I ♥ _____

_____

_____

_____

I love stopping to smell the roses,
literally & metaphorically—Ahhhh!

WhatDoULove? I ♥ _____

_____

_____

_____

*I love people. I love my family, my children...
but inside myself is a place I live all alone
and that's where you renew your springs that never dry up.*

— **Pearl S. Buck**

I love mornings when the day stretches out before me and my optimism is at its height.

WhatDoULove? I ♥ _____

_____

_____

_____

I love standing up for myself, for another, for what's right.

WhatDoULove? I ♥ _____

_____

_____

_____

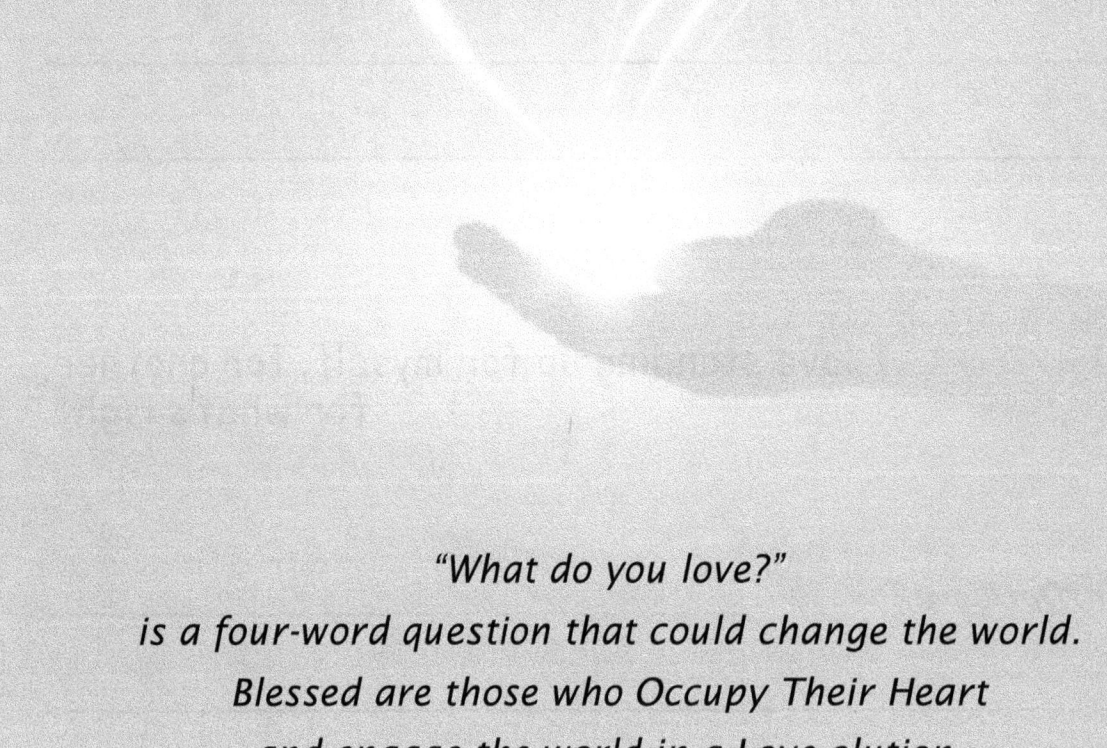

"What do you love?"
is a four-word question that could change the world.
Blessed are those who Occupy Their Heart
and engage the world in a Love-olution.

— I. J. Weinstock

— *A Love-olution* —
Cast a LoveSpell Over the World!

Our world is in the midst of a *Quickening*. The pace of change is accelerating so fast that we need a North Star to guide us through the profound upheavals rocking civilization's boat. Our most reliable compass is our capacity to love.

My New Year's resolution was to *beat the drum for love* to make 2012 The Year of Love. And for me it was! I deposited more than 1001 *LoveSpells* in my LoveBank and feel enriched as a result. I flew coast-to-coast more than a dozen times during the year and, due to my daily dose of Vitamin L, never caught a cold. I also traveled through time for love—three time-zones to be exact—moving from LA to NY to live with my new soul mate.

I believe in the power of love as expressed by the philosopher Teilhard de Chardin—"Some day, after we have mastered the winds, the waves, the tides and gravity, we shall harness the energies of love. Then, for the second time in the history of the world, mankind will have discovered fire."

I hope *The LoveSpell Secret* will inspire others to *Cast a Quantum LoveSpell* and grow the love in their lives. Through future books and media, more and more people will discover *The LoveSpell Secret* and become a part of this "Occupy the Heart" movement. When 144,000 people—young and old, men and women—*Occupy their Hearts*, a critical mass will be reached and it will become a Love-olution that *Casts A LoveSpell Over the World*!

Imagine what the world would be like if along with the billions of hamburgers sold, we cast a billion *LoveSpells*.

Now you know *The LoveSpell Secret*—Love is the answer AND the question! *What do YOU love?* Answer that question every day and you will not only discover the magical key to unlocking the treasure chest of your life, you will help heal and change the world.

CONGRATULATIONS
on
Casting a Quantum LoveSpell

Continue "beating the drum for Love" to grow the love in your life.

If you do, you'll be amazed by the magic that will occur.

WhatDoULove? I ♥ _____

_____

_____

_____

I love butterflies—as things of beauty
& symbols of transformation.

WhatDoULove? I ♥ _____

_____

_____

_____

I ♥

WhatDoULove? I ♥ _____

_____

_____

_____

I love the unusual,
and yet I'm comforted by the familiar.

WhatDoULove? I ♥ _____

_____

_____

_____

WhatDoULove? I ♥ _____
_____
_____
_____

I love holding a newborn &
marveling at the miracle of life.

WhatDoULove? I ♥ _____
_____
_____
_____

WhatDoULove? I ♥ _____

_____

_____

_____

I love being transported by a kiss.

WhatDoULove? I ♥ _____

_____

_____

_____

WhatDoULove? I ♥ _____

_____

_____

_____

I love standing in a summer rain—the original shower.

WhatDoULove? I ♥ _____

_____

_____

_____

WhatDoULove? I ♥ _____

_____

_____

_____

I love the 4-letter word SLOW—
it makes eating, breathing & loving better.

WhatDoULove? I ♥ _____

_____

_____

_____

WhatDoULove? I ♥ _____

_____

_____

_____

I love completing things
because it's so much harder than starting them.

WhatDoULove? I ♥ _____

_____

_____

_____

Acknowledgements

Every labor of love has many hands and hearts.

I want to thank April Hope Owen for hosting and facilitating the New Year's Eve drum circle where I received communication from Joy in the form of the question—*What Do You Love?*—which became the inspiration for this book.

I am deeply indebted to Dana Julien for throwing me into the deep end of the Twitter pool, confident that I'd learn to swim-tweet, which gave me a perfect medium for "beating the drum for love" and discovering the secret of *Casting a LoveSpell*.

I can't sing Dehanna Bailee's praises enough—she's every author's dream "book shepherd." Thank you for so skillfully mid-wifing *The LoveSpell Secret* into the world.

And finally, my profoundest gratitude goes to Lilly Julien for holding my hand and my heart, for her support and inspiration, and for the thousand and one new things she's taught me about love.

About the Author

I. J. "Jerry" Weinstock is the son of Holocaust survivors. During his varied career, he's been an actor, artist, producer and author. In the 80's, his groundbreaking book about women was featured on the *Donahue Show* (the Oprah of its time). In the 90's, his cable network, The Game Channel, was the precursor to GSN (The Game Show Network).

When Jerry lost his wife, Joy, to breast cancer, he was devastated. But a remarkable thing happened—Joy began communicating with him from the Afterlife. Over the course of a year, she led him on an incredible journey to heal his grief. Inspired by his extraordinary experience, he wrote a memoir, *JOYride: How My Late Wife Loved Me Back To Life*, which won an eLit Award—the Silver Medal for *Best Inspirational/Spiritual Digital Book* of 2011.

He has also written *Grief Quest: A Workbook & Journal to Heal the Grieving Heart* which was named a Finalist by the 2012 USA Best Book Awards.

On New Year's Eve 2011, while participating in a drum circle, his late wife, Joy, once again communicated with him from the Afterlife. She asked him a simple yet profound question—*What do you love?*—which became the inspiration for *The LoveSpell Secret: A 30-Day Heaven-Sent Program to Create More Love in Your Life.*

I. J. Weinstock lives in Los Angeles and New York, and can be reached at DreaMasterBooks@gmail.com or on Twitter @SoulmateGuider.

www.ingramcontent.com/pod-product-compliance
Lightning Source LLC
Chambersburg PA
CBHW080522110426

42742CB00017B/3202